Poetic

Signature v2

The **Deluxe** Edition

By R. T. Martin

RTM Publishing LLC

Poetic Signature: The Deluxe Edition

ISBN 978-1-7370213-4-6

Published by RTM Publishing LLC

Based in Apache Junction, Arizona

My Appreciation

First and foremost, I have to start by saying thanks be to Yahweh for everything. To be able to make a living writing and expressing myself to all of you is a gift unlike any other. Now with that being said, welcome to both the returning readers, as well as those who are seeing this title for the first time. Regardless of how you've come across this book, the fact that you've chosen to make time to read my poetry is more than flattering. I am both grateful and honored, and I hope that you'll be able to take away even more from what I have to offer.

Sincerely,
R. T. Martin

P.S. Adolescence (1-60) & Adulthood (61-107)

⇒

Table Of Contents

Welcome (Introduction)

Welcome to my thoughts please enjoy what you find.

For soon you will see, where others are blind.

I embrace with arms open, I invite with words true.

Come here where thoughts matter, this is my gift to you.

Clouds Over Stars

I prefer clouds over stars even though they don't
shine. I guess it's because we all know stars
burn out over time.

Although the same can't be said when it comes
to the clouds.

They love to travel, laze around, and even
huddle in crowds.

They cry when they feel weighed down, truly
expressive in fact. Afterwards they bless us with
a smile, letting a rainbow protract.

I wonder what it brings to mind when others see
clouds.

Do they try to form an image or feel loved ones
looking down? I'll let them speak their peace
leaving that question right there.

Next time you look up, see what they say to
you. I wonder what you'll hear.

My Heaven

Growing up I heard people speak of heaven,
They always made it sound like the place to be.
They referred to it as the land of milk and
honey,
Pearl gates and gold mansions for free.
They said it was a place with no more struggle.
They called it a true land of the free.
But I noticed in all those years of people talking,
No one ever asked what was heaven to me.

I picture halos lit from the sun's blessing rays.
Laughing with loved ones for infinite days.
And when the sun goes down we snuggle up to
stay warm,
Similar to a summer spot underblankets during a
cruel winter storm.
Oh how easily the mind forgets,
We're surrounded by all of our pets.

Just taking in the moments, breathtaking and timeless.
This is my picture of heaven, my vision of sublimeness.

To Think About Thought

I have come to realize the change in our minds.
While some things are mere coincidence others
are signs.
Yes I sat and thought on the topic of thought
until I considered the view.
I sat in this seat and looked at the trees through
the window then suddenly knew.
Our perspectives, our dreams, our crush from
our teens will continue to develop and change.
Our fashion, our food, even attitude will never
long to remain.
I asked myself why while time dwindled by
until a new thought had arrived. That to think
about thought was too much a thought for one
as mellow as I.
Instead I'll continually change despite looking
strange since I'd rather just do as I please. Yes
I'll grow and I'll change, and widen my range,
until I settle like these very trees.

Thoughts Like Craspedias

I want thoughts like craspedias, plentiful and
always full of light. The yellowness of optimism
stored within each bulb and held tight. I like to
spread a little joy, a pleasant sight you may say.
Keep in mind it adds up overtime," Rome
wasn't built in a day."

At times writing gets to feel old, yet I continue
my streak. Maybe I'll have a word for you when
you're down and feel you won't make it through
the week. I hope my words are like craspedias
unto all that read. Sometimes a little yellow in
your life is all that you need.

Color & Meaning

If I paint an orange blue what is it now to you?
Does the color change the core of what an
orange is?
I mean it seems obscene picturing greens no
longer green, like a black bean turning gin fizz.

I know the question may amuse and to some it
may confuse but all the same it haunted me as I
laid down in bed.
If we were all color blind how would we name
such things?
It's not like we go around calling apples reds.

I tend to ponder as I wander upon questions a
little yonder from what will actually help me as
I grow.
I can't help but get lost in such ridiculous
thoughts, maybe I'll start thinking less and just
go with the flow.

My Call Is

I was born into this world a writer.

History is my paper and success, my pen.

Sacred do I find my art, for every word holds
the potential to either create or destroy worlds.

When I look into the sky I see space.

Here is my home, the place beyond all my
enemies.

Although not secret it's hidden from all my
insecurities.

My mind travels and my hands simply write
what I have witnessed. What more can I say, my
call just... is.

The Importance of Glass

I once spoke to a glass of water, and started
asking if it was half empty or full. Can you
believe it left me without a reply? I thought I
had been a great audience, so all I could do was
question why.

To my surprise it had replied a bit later, the
answer given while I slept. Saying the
importance lies not in the water, but in the glass
that is kept.

Just like that glass we hold the future in its
entirety no madder its depth. Giving form to our
ideals with each and every step and breath.

Let Poetry Take You

There are many types of poets so go and take
your pick.
I myself like quite a few as well so find the one
whose poems stick.
To your spirit, to your truth, to the language that
you speak.

Love their style, love their content, treat their art
just like a feast. Consume their words, embrace
their feelings, let them become your very own.
Poetry is all over, let it take you into the vast
unknown.

Summit Haiku

On top a mountain
Tranquility resides here
The mind now unlocked

Pictures drawn from void
Till stories spill into thought
Emotions now flow

Haikus upon high
Ascended into freeverse feels
Creation echoes here

What Is Love

Love is an endless summer

and tenacious fairy tale,

connected to fathoms of pain.

A carousel of floating hearts and fire.

I've heard it said many times before, if you love them let them go. But I see partners like flowers, if you love them let them grow.
No need to rip them from the ground just to say they've been claimed. Let them blossom into their truth and admire what they've gained.

We all need time to become who we're meant to be, time will surely show. Sometimes we lose sight of this due to expectations, and also due to our ego.
I need not pick the flower I adore to know where it resides.
For even in a garden my flower always has my eyes.

Trying To Forget

I declare this the last straw, for I have had
enough. I've come to pay for your mistakes and
I shall call your bluff. I'll walk outside that
sunny door and find a new delight. For the heart
of the scorned is just too big a fight.

I won't miss a memory, no I won't miss a thing. I
will forget how you twirl your hair in circles
when you sing. I will forget the times you've
laughed when inside you longed to cry. I will
forget the times when we would watch the
morning sky.

Oh yes I will, oh yes I will, at least I sure shall
try. I'll walk away and pretend those days
haven't already gone by.

I must forget, must I forget, maybe I will just pretend? That the time we spent was all a dream, that you were never my friend.

Will I forget, can I forget, the things that we've been through? I do not think it can be done, for I'm already missing you.

Your sheepish laugh, your gentle touch, the complaining that you do. All these things have fallen in line, like I who've fallen for you.

So out that door shall I go, just to feel the breeze. And I expect to come back in to feel your loving squeeze.

Here's To Words Never Said

Memories dance in the night never seen, same
as flames for past lovers that are gone.
All truths left mute although they wish to
scream,
Now lies tears shed to a once joyous song.

For who am I to speak on how I feel?
I always let my actions speak for me.
Although my love is true my pride is real.
I will remain quiet yet crave for thé.

The world came into being through speech,
so this means in silence lies destruction.
Love just had too many lessons to teach,
I didn't care to heed its instruction.

I hold my memories close while in bed.
Awaiting love, here's to words never said.

I Am Yours

I'm used to giving my heart to many because
you are many in one.

When you speak you are the goddess of
euphony.

When you move, the empress of grace.

When you kiss me, the queen of tongues.

My heroine who has yet to be late.

Like a seeker from which I can't hide, better yet
an honor code or law for which I'll forever
abide.

I… am yours.

Woes of a Modern Tool

Crime is organized so like the criminal you are,

You played deliberate games that made me

mistake you for a star.

For my light,

My only right in a world full of wrong.

You sang me tales of love like gold,

And I danced to every song.

Oh so criminal is thé,

Who has played me for a fool.

Yet for you I still work day and night,

For I am just a tool.

Trust

I say what I know though I don't know much.
But what I do know is the purpose of trust.

Trust can be the faith you put in another.
Rather it be a stranger or your very own mother.

Trust is a chance you invest into someone.
Sometimes it's lost and at times it's won.

But we mustn't forget we must trust ourselves.
To get where we're headed, to stand where they
fell.

You see, I believe in the idea of trust.
To some it's for fools, but to me it's a must.

And I continue to chance it, because faith is
belief. And while living with trust, I'm filled
with relief.

How I Feel When In Love

This vibe that I'm in can't be held by physical
skin.
Left unexplained just to know it maintains my
happiness.

So if you may please consider this colorful
clarity that compliments the view.
Careless with clouded judgment only when I'm
with you.

Content with this contemporary state of
existence,
with foolish hopes that it never ends.

Just know that even when death separates us,
someday we'll be together again.

Abandonment

Like a man running to his doom
I let out cries and pleas.
Like the feeble man whose legs give way
I fall upon my knees.

Teardrops run like athletes or
rush like storming seas.
This is all I felt like when you
decided to just up and leave.

Sad Truth

She might already be taken,
But she has already taken my heart.
Although I wish her the best,
In the end I hope that they fall apart.

Because he'll never care the way that I care.
Because I've never shared this side of myself.
So I stay prepared for him to break her heart,
So I can be there to nurse her back to health.

Times of Yesterday

I don't know why our relationship has tight ties
with temporary goodbyes.
We try to taxi our separate ways and always end
up tandeming.
Two distraught tots sewn together like a
hemming.
Tons of tantrums, too many tireless talks. Taking
up for our faults when discussing them on our
walks.

There was a time our tale was topped with
tantalizing discussion.
Back when our communication didn't end with
terrible repercussions.
Moments full of tabu texts and tongue touches. I
wonder how we got here, we fell into murky
clutches.

I want to tiptoe to tomorrow where I can take you away.

To better times where we can get back what we had in our times of yesterday.

If You Choose To Love

Being in love brought out parts of me that I
never knew existed.
Most of the time it was bliss but there were
times I was twisted.
Sadly I didn't fall in love, no I chose this fate.
So when I yell I hate you, it's really me I hate.
Equivalent exchange, cashed in and got change.

My sunlight got brighter, my winters got colder.
My confidence grew, I became so much bolder.
The rocks that you threw all turned into
boulders.
Yet I learned to stand tall while leaning on your
shoulder.

Love is sacrifice, it enhances emotion. Turning
our simple tears into waves of an ocean.
No matter what you do, no matter the notion...

Choose who you love wisely, know it comes with commotion.

Happy Birthday Ma

I had another poem in mind but this meant much
more. That's because at heart who this poem is
meant for. This is for the queen that brought me
into this life. The lioness that always worked to
provide. My example for what makes a proper
wife and the one in whom I can always confide.

Sorry for the times I made you worry, and for
the times that I rebelled.
After all of your love and sacrifice you are truly
a sight to be beheld. I think back to when I was
a knee height small pint stealing all of your
socks. I admire how you are exemplary and
have always remained my rock. I want the
world to know that I am honored to have you as
my mother.
May you have a wonderful birthday, and
another, and another.

Happy birthday ma, ♥ Roy

Chasing Clouds

Make a habit of chasing clouds and you'll miss
out on the sun. We tend to focus on what we
want and not what has come. A new horizon, a
newer plane, something yet to explore. The
endless wanting and aimless walking leaves
some crawling for more. But where does it stop,
where do we settle, where is the comfort once
known? The need to be in need has left us
without home. No place to rest when you want
the best although there will always be better. To
chase the chase in an endless race, society of the
self inflicted debtor.

Gaining & Maintaining

The key is to maintain, so practice consistency
in authenticity. You can't afford to live a life not
of your own accord. In the end there's no reward
for living a lie.
So I advise that you shine in all of your truth,
you deserve to live honestly before you die.

We've never been promised tomorrow, it's fair
to say we're not even promised today. So with
each and every moment that you take breath,
choose to live this your own way. To the fullest
when feeling empty and on the brightside when
in the dark. I know that you'll find your way,
now go out and leave your mark.

Humility & Revelations

So many lessons of humility found while in the dirt.

So many tears never shed despite feeling hurt.

I searched to find a peace of mind but it was never found, because instead of going within I chose to look around.

But times have changed, I did the work and now it's paying off. I now take pride within my growth while others may scoff.

I've learned that life is like a wave and I'm content with flowing. Wide smile in the sunlight with my teeth showing.

Head high even when I don't know where I'm going, because there's adventure to be had in the midst of not knowing. No longer addicted to complication or badgered with my temptations. Constantly receiving blessings and coming into revelations.

Message to Self

Ignore when others say that your wait is in vain,
because before tremendous blessing comes
sacrifice and pain.

Life is flowerful, embrace its pedals and its
thorns.

There's no need to masquerade like angels when
we all have our horns.

So be patient with yourself, don't judge progress
by time.

Know that you're up to the task and you'll be
more than fine. Cast aside appearances, don't
worry how long your journey takes. Remember
to always love yourself more than any of your
mistakes.

Fitting In Vs Belonging

Just like a size twelve foot in a size ten shoe,
you blend and pretend when it only hurts you.
Just because it's the norm doesn't make it for
you.
Shrinking to fit in because of insecurities you
grew.
What will they think and how will you look?
It doesn't matter when you're the author of your
life, the writer of your book.
Think too critical on the thoughts of critics and
you'll lose your spark. The light you hide inside
that guides others out of the dark. This foolish
act will strike you back and you'll lose the
person you once knew. Because when all the
eyes are gone even the mirror won't be able to
find you.
It's not a crime to fit so please don't get me
wrong.

Just make sure you're not just fitting in, make sure you're where you belong.

Happy Or Free

I was taught that there's a difference between
being happy and being free. Because to those
that know no better captivity is thé. To have no
need for thinking, a simple path laid out.
Knowing exactly what lies ahead, free of
decisions and doubt. To be free is to have power
and being powerful can feel strange. Some
would rather live without it in hopes that their
lives will never change. Like the student afraid
of graduation, better yet the choices to be made.
Some people find happiness in deterring growth,
remaining on a single stage.

More Loss Than Gain

Let us not drink the drink of drunkards to find
ourselves anew. Maybe I should put this bottle
down and rid my thoughts of you.

Let us not dance the dance of fools for passion
can be cruel. To twist and turn till our souls burn
in a bed of desire's rule.

Let us not embrace the what ifs and what nots
that haunt us as we walk. The great temptations
that lurk within us despite the good we talk.

Let us not be one in the name of fun, for what
lies ahead is pain. No matter how much pleasure
may await, the loss out numbers the gain.

The Story of Job

What be thy will for me oh lord, do my cries fall
upon deaf ears? Have my acts of reverence
amount to naught despite the toilsome years?
Am I to be the afflicted and thrown among the
chaff? Am I to bear only sorrow, denied both
smile and laugh?
The weakness in me shown through questions I
have asked. These very same questions which I
have long masked.
Wondering about my choices while pondering
my path.
Yet still I stand steadfast, with sweat and tears
as my bath.

Patience

I've spoken of patience before but I've been
lacking it of late. At times my want for results
brings me tournament while I wait. To achieve
and rejoice in all that I see. This is my goal and
at times it haunts me.

But alas I've sat and noticed what rushing gets.
Frustration, disappointment, and even regrets.
I've been working, I've been thinking, I've been
tiring out.
So I've stepped back and reset because I live on
faith and not doubt.

I'm getting where I need to be no matter how
slow. Obstacles come amply but that's what
happens when you grow. I'm now going to take
my time and let things circulate and flow. It's all
working out, this is something that I know.

Let It Out

Kings and queens smile ear to ear with watery eyes, label them tears of joy because weakness is unacceptable.

It's not befitting of royals to cry, don't you know that sadness is detestable?

Head high, pain is myth, hurt doesn't exist.

Never show when you're tired, in fact you're never tired, I'm sure you get the gist.

At least that's what we're taught when in truth that's nonsense. A bad day deserves a good vent session. And to cry is quite respectable, afterwards you can seek to refreshen.

Let out the pain there's more to gain after you let it go.

Emotion doesn't make you weak, it just goes to show. We go through struggles then overcome, there's beauty in this fact. Don't let stress build up like clothing, you only feel the weight after it's been packed.

Uphill

It's a long way to go but such a beautiful
journey, this is constant throughout life.
And although this may sound quite odd, you
must come to terms with all of its strife.
Similar to after a storm comes a rainbow, after
climbing a hill comes the view.
Know that after all of the struggle you'll look
back with content knowing that you made it
through.
Yes it sucks during the battle regardless of if it's
external or not, but you're meant to jump
hurdles so remember what you've got. You have
power unseen yet present, subtle but strong no
less.
Resilience unlike any other which is why you
need not stress. Climb this hill, take your time,
and show to all what you can do. Although
remember that each journey is unique, so make
sure that it's worth it to you.

JALAPENO

Just take a breath and

Accept that perfection is overrated.

Life is a journey so embrace the ride.

As you find your way in this wacky world

Personal growth is key, so prioritize

Evolving into the rawest form of yourself.

Not all opportunities are meant to be. The

Obligation you hold is simply to be you.

The Beauty of the Backflip

Stare in awe of the backflips's beauty because
while looking effortless it takes so much to
complete.
And no matter how many times we repeat it,
we'll still never truly master its nature.
It's steps consisting of our day to day lives, but
all in the blink of an eye.
We feel the waters catching our ideal flow,
preparing to do more. Which leads to the lift off,
exiting our comfort zone in hopes of success.
The turn from which we let go of all doubt and
then the drop, flop, fall, and stumble until we
finally land it.
In that moment all of our work and failure pays
off leaving us to reap the fruits of our labor.
From gymnasts to the average Joe the backflip
remains somewhat of an anomaly because even
if not physically, we repeat this act with every
decision throughout our lives.

The never ending cycle is simply the everlasting backflip.

Here's to Eighteen

Here's to my last summer as a kid, may these times serve me well. Honoring trials where I rose along with all the times I fell.
I'm in no rush to be great, just enjoying my time.
I'm a tad all over the place but it's working just fine.
Today I've turned eighteen, today I have transcended.
I'm becoming the man I'm meant to be, the time for waiting has ended.
Although life isn't too much different since I stay true to being me.
The ambitious truth seeker who lives to be free.

This Generation

Hello and goodbye young fragile minds.

Heaven's beauty and Earth's devine.

Wisdom's student and hero's victim.

Under a system made to cripple,

served with laws to trick them.

Oh great bottles filled with content.

Their thoughts race, this they do constant.

Some feel to love and others to condem.

Surrounded by foes though somehow find
friends.

They do as they think and think as they're told.

So who's mind does power truly behold?

Siren's Gaze

The realest poetry known to man are words of
truth.
Honesty from the heart are facts without need of
proof.
So honestly speaking I feel as if I'm captivated
by the siren's gaze.
Though my mind sees clearly my body still
strays.
Am I a broken man who returns to his ways?
Or just another trier going through one of those
days?
He who suffers from an addiction whatever it
may be.
Probably drugs, love of money, or even too
much fantasy.
Because that's the purpose of addiction you
know?
Escaping reality's hash ways and so.

Its tide of unpleasantries all washed away, while
hypnotized by the sirens that gaze my way.

Changed Heroes

I know the story of how greed changed a dream.
From a diamond in the rough to a star in the
gleam.
When wealth a silent pleasure and titles are
whores.
When laughter brings about sorrow and success
no rewards.
For whom should they pity the poor or the rich?
The scrappers and scrapers or those dead in a
ditch?
The murderer scared of losing slaver, or the
brave who die in their sense of bravery.
For they no longer know who is to blame.
The lamb to the slaughter or the wolf who has
slain.
The corruption they consume or the corruptors
they uphold.
Those who were strong, whose faith has grown
cold.

Followers

There's irony in the fact that what most aspire to be is a clone of a servant.

They formed through false teachings like mass produced dolls, while some stay observant.

Watching the slow but steady change as their minds become deranged, what was once considered proper is now what's strange.

Their false sense of accomplishment only shows their hidden scars.

The fact that they don't accept the truth, just shows they don't know who they are.

Define Time

Tell me what is time to you,
is it the ticking of the clock?
The wrinkles in one's flesh
or the pause in one's thoughts?
Tell me what I do not know,
what I have come to find.
We talk so much about it yet
lack the words to define.
Through it what is gained,
through it what is lost?
A treasure without price
yet a beauty that can cost.

Without Home

Who is more unfortunate than those without
home?
Without bed to lay, simply fated to roam.
The wondering wanderers who drift by day,
embrace only by night as their place to stay.

Broken Glass

Why is it that our darkest days usually invoke
creativity?
Art created from sunless places yet somehow
producing light.
Like glass breaking in order to form an image.
While it no longer tends to its initial function, its
existence can now stand for more.
Now it can become a symbol to bring about
different perspectives.
I guess we too relate to glass.
We vary in size, tint, and purpose.
Some of us see through, some of us bullet proof,
some of us broken.
Yet we all can bring about different perspectives
and can stand for more if we allow it.

Domestic

I put my ear to the door and hear fuss.

Thunderous anger thrown without restrain.

Talk of broken word sprinkled with ruined trust.

Her voice echoing with a distinct pain.

He tries to calm her storm yet to no avail.

Her arms just flailing both this way and that.

Tears pour like rain and fury create great hail.

All her thoughts of reason just seem to scat.

You've made an imbecile of me, my heart.

Shattered hopes now float in the atmosphere.

She stands ready to tear my father apart.

Maybe I should act like I did not hear.

The camel's back break in my family.

Woe is now here, along with calamity.

Confessions

Today I ran into a problem of my trade.
Determining what I should keep private and
what's meant to be displayed.
When I write I always do so from the heart,
I like to be authentic when it comes to my art.
But today I wrote a poem that left me feeling
almost naked.
As if meant to be secret, I dare say sacred.
I know myself, I'm not ashamed of anything I
feel.
Yet this poem makes me question how much
should be revealed.
Is there a line between exposed and expression?
Sometimes these poems feel less like poems,
and more like confessions.

The Folly of Youth

I want to have some fun and act dumb,

make choices I know I'll regret.

Then blame it on my youth,

say experience is what I was trying to get.

I want to be reckless and act out of character

because that's what it means to be free.

I hear it's all apart of the process,

you know the one to find the inner me.

They tell me yolo, live it up, and enjoy it while I

can.

Live for sexual conquest and wreck my health

just to feel like I'm a man.

I'm too young to know true love, too young to

settle down.

Too young to know myself, yet just of age to

fool around.

If I see things differently I'm judgmental and

out of touch.

I was told these are the days to make mistakes,

although we've seen them happen all too much.

Missing Home

Memories of sweet Saturday mornings back
home will never fade. Friendships and moments
more exquisite than the finest jade. Alongside
playing music from the marching band stands.
Or even our lunch table where worries shrank
into sand.

I guess what I mean to say is that home will
always be home. Even though I left I still
remember the place from where I've grown.

I didn't foresee missing it this much, I've never
been one to grow attached. You don't see chicks
crying to return to the eggs from which they
hatched. But in truth "Reading" is comfort, from
its corner stores to its beaten roads. I miss
watching the sun rise above the hills, and even
shoveling snow in truckloads.

I know this isn't the time for longing since I'm
far away. In my heart I know that I'll return
although as for when I can not say. I know that

I'm just reminiscing and missing my family and my friends. For now I'll just smile thinking of when I'll see them all again.

The Power of Poetry

When I listen to certain poets speak I'm left in awe.

I hear truths that shine light on mankind's every flaw.

Pictures painted with imagery clearer than my reflection.

Sermons so deep afterwards I'm in need of reflection.

Questioning my ability, how far can I go?

What separates poetic cliche from a lyrical pro?

What makes a man a man, what makes him worth his salt?

Why do we have dominion over the earth when we are filled with fault?

They birth so many profound questions within me that I'm always left dazed.

I guess the power of poetry is simply to leave those who feel it amazed.

Viewing A King

I see splendor in waves as I view a king.

Although he bears no crown and wears no ring.

His carriage nowhere to be found and no vast
riches seen.

Yet he is a king for it's all in his genes.

From before his father's father he had owed his
throne.

Because principles passed down since before
them, were to become his very own.

To be a man worth his salt setting goals, despite
a fool's errand they seem.

Always showing quality in his work and in
pursuit of his dreams.

I let the water hit my face after I close my eyes.

And when I open them to no surprise I see a
king staring back at me.

Front Seat View (New Introduction)

Some people like poems that leave a little to the imagination.
I like to say exactly what I mean, because I meant exactly what I said.
No need to run around in circles getting my truth misconstrued until you find yourself misled.
It's rather simple.
As a poet I express what I feel.
I share what I have felt.
Sometimes I'm moaning about heartbreak or venting about the cards I've been dealt.
Then there are times I'm trying to be uplifting, I tell who listens a point of view.
You might not relate to everything, but hopefully you learn from a few.
I'm not a poet for the public, although sharing my poetry is something I do. At the end of the day every page is me venting, you're just getting a front seat view.

Poetic Jumping

As I stand between the bookshelves of the
poetry section losing myself in the insecurities
of others, I hear a rattling.
There's a constant shake and cry from the
books as if they're unrest won't cease until
they attack.
Oh I can picture it now, the poetry volumes
have been discussing the need for new works.
What better way to initiate new blood than
through a good old fashioned game of "fight
back"?
Either that or the ceiling is plotting to collapse
on me any second now.
Maybe it aims to bury me here for eternity,
lost among the voices of the talented and the
honest.
I wonder if these shelves will one day claim
me as well. God knows, I pray they do.

Pride In Limitation

A life with no limits,

Is a ride in which you lose yourself.

Think about it,

This body alone has its needs.

Water, food, air, and rest.

How can we live limitless in a vessel meant for temporary use?

Not to mention,

What is limitless living?

Ample sex and drug abuse?

Is it adrenaline rushes everyday or delicacies galore?

Limitless living is usually a front for living like teens that ignore their chores.

No idea of the bigger picture,

Focused only on what the eyes can see.

Opinions and competition, living in the moment until it leads to agony.

This doesn't mean don't overcome.

This is not an excuse not to be great.

I'm just giving sound advice because I've observed many and seen their fate.

One who thinks they're without limits, is already as lost as the crowd.

Set your limitations wisely,

And in those boundaries be proud.

Forced Learner

I have no experience loving someone else the
way that I love you.

You know, altering my point of view and
yanking hope out of a hat.

But there was also a time before that, and
experience found me as you could say.

So don't force me to learn this lesson, I fear I
don't know how to rue the day.

And if anything, I'm quite scholarly in fact.

For me, mastery is inevitable, I was born a class
act.

The Affliction of the Genuine

It's been a while since I've picked up a pen.

Devastated, I've been told I'm too ideal once again.

Apparently I deserve someone better, unrealistic in fact.

It seems I give so much away, they don't know what to give back.

I wonder when being genuine was sought after, now it's abnormal at best.

Back then this used to anger me, at times I swelled with regret.

It's bittersweet loving wholly, the traumatized get scared.

But I refuse to love any other way, at least they know that I cared.

Twenty Years

Twenty years on this mystical mystery rock.

Been through at least twenty phases.

Some cold & others hot.

Blooded, tempered, sweat, and flashes.

Twenty years down and who knows how many
more to go.

I wonder if I'd be better off fast or slow.

To act, commit, forgive, anger.

Oh the answer I may never know, but what more
can I expect.

I've spent twenty years on this floating rock and
haven't gotten a clue yet.

New Perspective

The more I look at my poetry,

The more I take pride in what I write.

Where I once saw my words as too simple,

I now see them as direct.

And what I once perceived as common knowledge,

I now see as gems for the willing.

New Perspective Extended

The more I look at my poetry,

The more I take pride in what I do.

Where I once saw my words as too simple,

I now see them as direct.

And what I once perceived as common knowledge,

I now see as gems for the willing.

I say willing, not smart, because I've seen foolish geniuses.

I say willing, not wise, because I know far too many wise men who choose carnally.

You can't live through a book

And despite all your knowledge you're bound to come across a subject in which you're unfamiliar.

In such cases, those who are willing to listen and learn prosper.

As for the rest, they fall into the same trap as the ones before them.

I'm not a prophet, just an honest man.

Honestly, honesty itself is sometimes too powerful to bear.

So to those who are willing to listen.

I thank you for lending me your ear.

I pray my truths help make your path a little more clear.

Potential Harm

Potential is dangerous, its potency varies and can leave addiction.

"If only they did this, they'd be what I need.

If I walk away now, I'd have abandoned that seed.

Of hopes and dreams planted when we were just teens.

Clueless about reality, trying to figure out our schemes."

See I've spoken of sweet releases,

Tethered with tragic goodbyes,

but it has long been time to let potentiality die.

Because at the day's end,

Potential is power untapped.

Maybe it's left that way for a reason,

And you should just leave it at that.

The Blessing

I stopped chasing once I realized I'm the blessing, not a prize.

I am more than an asset, I am growth in disguise.

Understand the first is divine, the gift that keeps giving.

The second is merely a day's reward to be forgotten while living.

I can't be won through a single effort, then kept with neglect.

You need to show me consistency, or with my loss you'll be met.

Oh if only you knew, how close you stood to the day,

when you lost the very helper that God had sent your way.

But it's not too late, although it's very close in fact.

To the point where there will be no light to guide your way back.

God made the world in seven days, he made everything right.

So I give you just a week till we bid our story it's final goodnight.

Like I said, I stopped chasing once I realized I'm the blessing, not a prize.

Because when I bless someone else, you better not be surprised.

D. A. M. N.

Damn I am great.

Dramatic, addictive, moral, and not with the nonsense.

I lay back and watch memories, I grew tired of movies a ways ago.

Speaking of ways, I don't know which way to go.

Maybe I'll tumble into trouble, or parade into paradise.

Slide into some scandal, then disco out of the disaster.

What do you expect, when adventure lurks behind every choice.

I promise I'll get where I'm meant to be, when I'm meant to be there.

And when I arrive I'll exhale and say it again.

Damn, I am great.

Today's Tea

Today the tables turn.

Talk turns to true transparency.

Take time to taste tacfullness's tantalizing tang

Trough training to tame the temperament.

Tether to the truthful to topple trife.

Tell troublemakers to take their tall tales to the trash.

Turn to total transcendence today.

Not Just Anyone

Not everyone can do this, be wise enough to
know they know nothing.

Or smart enough to view intelligence as a tool.

Blue enough to be a source of strength for those
in need.

And caged enough to seek freedom, yet free
enough to set boundaries.

I'm telling you, not everyone can do this.

Good thing I'm not just anyone.

Breaking Down Pain

Use those down times to elevate.

Turn hurt into triumph and terror to thrill.

This way, not only do those moments have
purpose,

but you'll see pain as nothing but an acronym.

Patiently acquiring intellectual nourishment.

Lionheart

Two decades down and my spirit hasn't
changed,

because even though I've learned a lot,

this lionheart still remains.

BARS...(jk)

Trash & Treasure

Answer me this, can you properly tell trash from treasure?

Although it sounds black and white it all comes down to how you measure.

You see we weigh options off perspective although people soon find,

that misvalue is a deception unlike any other kind.

It can make you take a joker for a king and the wiser for a clown.

Or have you trade your shekels for shackles and throw away your crown.

In short a man that can't see value will fall prey to those who can.

Imagine owning a private island and only valuing a grain of sand.

1986 Love

If I say I love you like my Cadillac, know that it's beyond the norm.

A love from before my conception, so true even before I was born.

Flawed but without deception, yet highly contradictory.

Because even if broken, the wholesomeness never fades.

Every crack, stain, and dent serves as our history.

A love beyond innocent's plane.

Regardless of if we're reclining like her seats or flying down memory lane, this love is eternal and without disdain.

Why I Don't Write

It's unusual for me to write without pain.

So if I'm poemless for a while just wish me
luck.

It's not that I pray these hands won't grace a pen
again.

I just hope my motivation comes from a better
space.

Please pray I keep all the joy that I obtain,

Sometimes danger can't reach you when you're
stuck.

We all need to kick back every now and then.

As life is meant to be lived in the first place.

B-ball With A Stranger

Today I played b-ball with a stranger.

It was a workout through and through.

Crazy crossovers, keeping low to the ground.

Could've dribbled in between my legs, but instead I zipped around.

It was great, oh I'm telling you the moment was hot.

At least that was until I missed, matter of fact I missed a lot.

I'm talking from the foul line to lay up hops.

I said I played b-ball with a stranger, whether I was good, I did not.

But there's more to the story than missing.

There's more to sports than being the best.

It's about spirit, it's about effort, life is checkers not chess.

You won't out smart every opponent, you won't make every shot.

But if you place your heart in every move, you'll leave every obstacle chopped.

The Best Time To Shop

For the first time in five years I walked the isles
of a store in peace.

Usually I feel the stares, I hear the unsaid as I
pass.

I tap aimlessly at my phone, hoping the
shunning won't last.

Eventually I learned to lean on loved ones for
comfort.

I couldn't checkout without someone on call.

But today was different, I didn't feel fear at all.

Music blasting as I made my way to the chips.

I swerved around shopping carts, jamming
while making my rounds.

Just flowing among the rows surrounded by
uplifting sounds.

The source of my strength was unexpected, the day after my world had stopped.

Who knew shopping after heartbreak, was the greatest time to shop.

Just A Message for Today

On a park bench, hair down, playing D.M.B. as the wind blows.

I'm taking in the day as time passes me by.

Just thinking, somewhere, someone is suffering.

Someone is facing the very worst moment of their life.

Meanwhile I'm sitting in peace watching bunnies play, simply grateful for the day.

This may not count as a poem, but there's a message I have to say.

Go outside and let the sun caress your skin for a change.

Take in the moment because life is fleeting as we focus on the temporary.

In this life of war, take every ounce of peace existence has to offer.

Take nothing for granted, because we never know when we will face the worst.

What She Told Me

I once asked her if she finds me to be weak, is a
man allowed to show his heart?

It feels weird expressing myself so much, am I
not playing my part?

Don't get me wrong, I can be stern, I know how
to be mighty too.

But when I'm with my girl, becoming putty is
all that I can do.

So I told her to be straight, is it a turn off when
I'm at ease.

She smiled for a moment, she loves to be a
tease.

She said my weakness shows my strength, and that I make her feel safe.

She loves that I'm a fighter who loves wholly, and how I give without restraint.

She then paused and told me not to bother thinking about how I'm seen.

That's when I smiled back at her, I knew I had found my queen.

The Look

I remember one day in my senior poetry class. My teacher told me I had the looks of a poet. My locks flowed down and my leather jacket glistened under the lights. But there was something missing. Although the words came out, the truth hid behind my cool exterior. He said my heart just wasn't there. It's been four years since that day, and I just understood what he meant.

Afraid, too afraid to express my pain although brave enough to share. Even though my poems told the story of my life, my pride made me remain closed off. They could never know my struggle, the hurt of a lover forced to fight. The pain of the wanderer. They could never know… me.

Love Throughout Media

We share a love that transcends media.

You are my Tali and I, your Shepard.

I'm your gentle Legoshi and you, my hardened
Haru.

The Bertie to my Speckle as I the Warden to
your Morrigan.

Night and day but far from good and evil.

Just two wholes that were made for eachother.

For You and Them

The hardest love is when you can't bring
yourself to fault them, even when they're
wrong.

You think back to their pain and tell yourself
everythings ok, for them you must be strong.

But don't lose yourself to their sadness, you
can't help if you're dead weight.

Partners help each other with their problems by
balancing, can't put too much on one slate .

It's ok to be there for them, you can love with
all your might.

But you must hold the ones you love
accountable, or they lose sense wrong and right.

Always remember it takes two whenever there is love, you're not in it by yourself.

Be sure to sit them down when needed, and prioritize your mental health.

Jungle Pot Plot

If I poison you slowly you'll love me for it, but
if I shoot a man I'll be condemned.

The same as rappers poisoning the art by
posing, as gangsters who shed blood to defend.

Their names, homes, and codes given by those
who were tricked.

Thinking their lives were better this way while
their throats were getting slit.

Rappers rap and give a dream, which a young
child will claim.

That kid shapes his hopes around the lies
thinking that life's without pain.

Poisoned by petty tales he puts his fellow man
down, then corrupts the innocence of his women

because he's been taught that's what it means to
be brown.

But in the end, how can I hate the popular teller
of tales?

He too was fed the same lies and has nothing
else if he fails.

Once again another child left victim of a plot,
set to trap our royalty in the heartless jungle pot.

False History

As a child hearing "my history" evoked in me a
rage,
Because instead of my history I was given a
stage.
A place of actors, blurred events, and mistold
tales.
One where I'm misguided and the truth is freed
to no avail.

Because when you hear black you think slavery
and rap.
Why don't you think of Queen Amanirenas and
how she pushed the Romans back?
We're taught we only kill each other and don't
know our worth,
But they don't dare to mention Black Wall
Street and the atrocities of 1921, May 31st.

Why do they promote black athletes while
trying to erase black kings?
Why do they label me harshly and associate my
color with only ignorant things?
I've been given identical idols meant to lead me
astray,
Then told to march with my oppressors saying
that everything will be ok.

You see this isn't all about the falsehoods by
which they abide.
It's more about the truth my perpetrators hide.
We come from greatness but they'd rather say
we come from slaves.
And they prioritize that we think this until they
send us to our graves.

Normalcy After the Fact

It's funny how we change to feel loss less.

We start going out of our element to forget how normalcy feels.

Like how it's normal for them to call when you reply to their good morning text.

Or how you make fun of them when they're unsuspecting.

We try to shake ourselves loose from the fact that they were a part of our world.

So our world is what we begin to reject.

I felt more confident for a day and then I felt even more free on the next.

After that I almost broke while watching a children's movie.

Currently I'm on the verge of the question, "what now?"

Has my world permanently changed, or will things go back to normal?

Separations are pretty peculiar that way, aren't they?

Vodka and Sage

Don't ask me why but at night I like to burn
sage.

Maybe it's the aroma or something on a spiritual
page.

I hear it clears the mind, oh isn't that serene?

Too bad tomorrow night I'm chugging vodka till
I dream.

Well not exactly, it's more like until I'm honest.

Five minutes after the sixth shot and truth
stumbles in as promised.

I like to get deep in thought and as expressive as
can be.

Probably the sage I'll burn the following day
will wash away the honesty.

Poem From Out of The Bottle

I'm not drunk enough, this form is a lie.

A disguise as drunk, that sobriety hides.

I want my truths to pour like vodka in my
double shot.

Troubling to some but to me the drink is not.

I just want to be honest, I want to vent to a
friend.

You see now I understand too what a drunkard
comprehends.

The drink is about honesty, the drink is a friend.

A bitter truth to a truthful end.

You see this isn't enough, I need just a bit more.

Till I find the honesty that I'm searching for.

I want to dissolve the barrier that holds the tongue.

Even if it's unwanted there are tales to be sung.

In this moment I'm genius, I am quick with a pen.

Let me show you my wisdom the bottle helped send.

I hope you listen and if so listen well.

Because here are words of the fearless that dwell.

In a world of lies be true, in a world of hate find love.

If you were born to fight, then fight

but only for what's worth fighting of...

I meant over, like the overbearing task of life.

Hold on and find what makes life worth living.

Take on ye a husband or a wife.

On this journey you'll find many things,

I know not the wonders you'll find.

But as for my search, love is beautiful and blind.

I long for my companion, may her hand come to my side.

May she blind me from the boredom and love me for all time.

In boredom comes vulnerability, we search for anything to cure.

Feet go where they're not meant to, impurity sneaks upon the pure.

Just love, and love them true. Let them keep that boredom at bay.

But make sure they love you, and keep close so that they stay.

Don't falter in your duty when their heart has become yours.

Love is a beauty but it's also a chore.

Embrace, sing, and cherish for it doesn't come everyday.

Embrace, love, and cherish, may you both always stay this way

Meet the Author

R. T. Martin is an author, poet, and entrepreneur born and raised in Reading, Pennsylvania. The teen author of yesterday is now a full-fledged adult, yet again testing the bounds of his creativity. When away from his keyboard you can find him either in the gym, or in bed binge watching cartoons and romcoms to his heart's content.

Be sure to check out our assortment of handcrafted jewelry and natural soaps on our website (rtmpublishing.com). All purchases not only help to fund future publications, but also help us to give back to our supporters.

You can keep up with all publications and future events from anywhere.

Website:rtmpublishing.com

Instagram.com/rtmpublishing

Twitter.com/rtmpublishing

TikTok.com/rtmpub

Thank you again for purchasing this book and any for helping support what started as a childhood fantasy. I am grateful to everyone who has helped pave the way towards where we're heading.

Made in the USA
Middletown, DE
16 November 2022

14948736R00071